Contents

Hola (Hello)

Hola, me llamo María. ¿Cómo te llamas?

Me llamo Rafael.

Hola	Hello
Buenos días	Good morning
Buenas tardes....................	Good afternoon
Me llamo	My name is
¿Cómo te llamas?	What is your name?
¿Cómo estás?	How are you?
Muy bien............................	very good
Regular...............................	so so
Mal......................................	not good
Adiós	Good bye

¿Cómo estás? (How are you?)

Muy bien

Regular

Mal

In Spanish questions start with an upside down question mark.

Adiós (Good bye)

¿Cómo te llamas? (What is your name?)

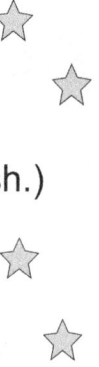

1) Preséntate a ti mismo en español. (Introduce yourself in Spanish.)

¿Cómo te llamas?
Me llamo Inma.

Tell Inma your name by writing **me llamo** followed by your name.

Me llamo _ _ _

_____ _____ _____   .

2) Sigue las líneas. ¿Qué dicen los niños?
Follow the lines. What do the children say?

a)

b)

c)

Antonio
Carlos
Juan
Rosa
Carmen

d)

e)

Me llamo Carlos.

a) _____ .

b) _____ .

c) _____ .

d) _____ .

e) _____ .

The double l
in Spanish
sounds like
an English y.

So try saying
me llamo as if
it was me yamo

Remember
though to write
it as me llamo .

2

¿Cómo estás? (How are you?)

muy bien - very good   regular - so so   mal - not good

Mira a las personas y escribe cómo están.
(Look at the people and write how they are feeling.)

a)

regular

b)

_____

c)
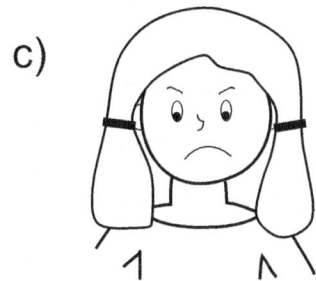

_____

d)

_____

e)
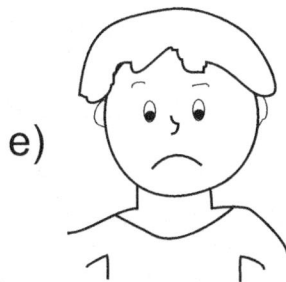

_____

f)

_____

g)

_____

h)

_____

Buenos días

Buenos días ....Good morning
Buenas tardes .... Good afternoon
Buenas noches ....Good evening / night
Por favor ....Please
Gracias ....Thank you
Sí..Yes
No .... No
Hasta luego ....See you
Adiós ....Good bye

Sigue las líneas para ver qué dicen los niños.
(Follow the lines to see what the children are saying.)

a) Spanish word _____ *adiós* 🖉
   _____

   English meaning _____ *Good bye*
   _____

b) Spanish word _____

   English meaning _____

c) Spanish word _____

   English meaning _____

d) Spanish word _____

   English meaning _____

por favor

adiós

gracias

Buenas tardes

Sopa de letras (wordsearch)

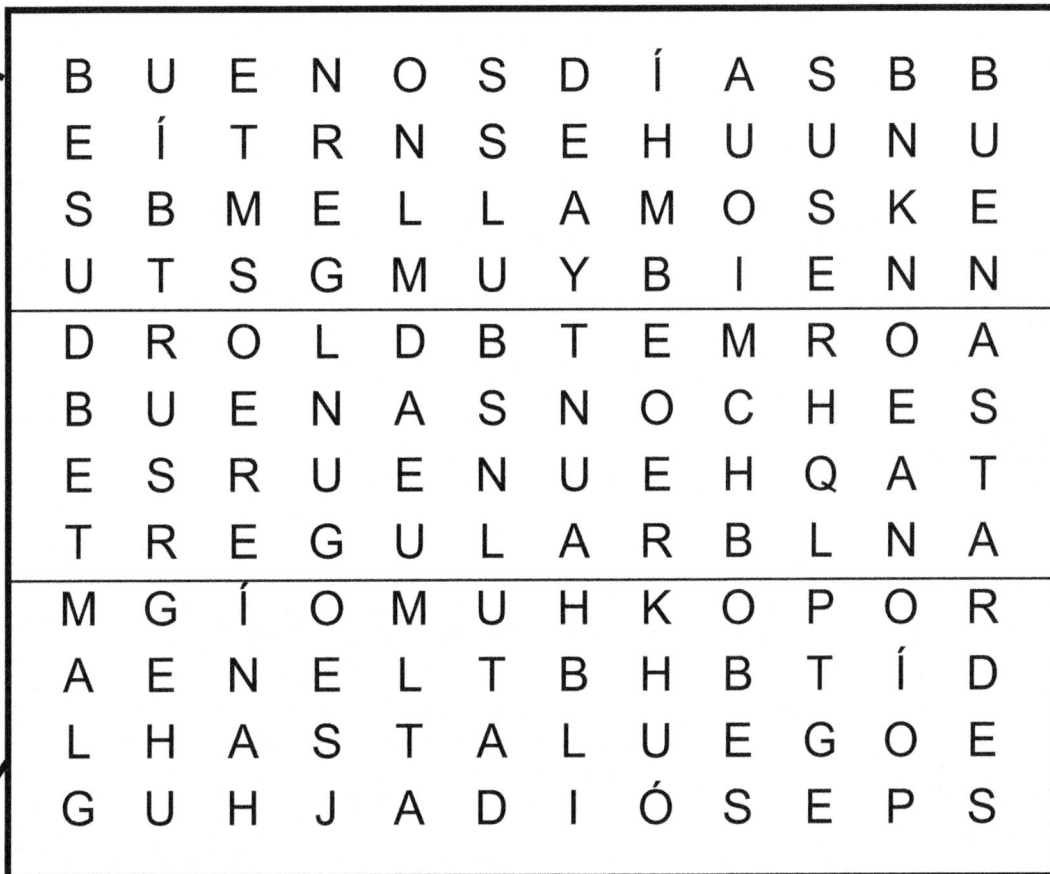

```
B U E N O S D Í A S B B
E Í T R N S E H U U N U
S B M E L L A M O S K E
U T S G M U Y B I E N N
D R O L D B T E M R O A
B U E N A S N O C H E S
E S R U E N U E H Q A T
T R E G U L A R B L N A
M G Í O M U H K O P O R
A E N E L T B H B T Í D
L H A S T A L U E G O E
G U H J A D I Ó S E P S
```

Busca estas palabras. (Look for these words.)

HOLA	ME LLAMO
BUENOS DÍAS	MUY BIEN
BUENAS TARDES	REGULAR
BUENAS NOCHES	MAL
HASTA LUEGO	SÍ
ADIÓS	NO

 diez

 uno

 nueve

 dos

 ocho

Los números

 tres

 siete

 seis

 cinco

 cuatro

Los números (numbers)

Rellena los números que faltan.
(Fill in the missing numbers.)

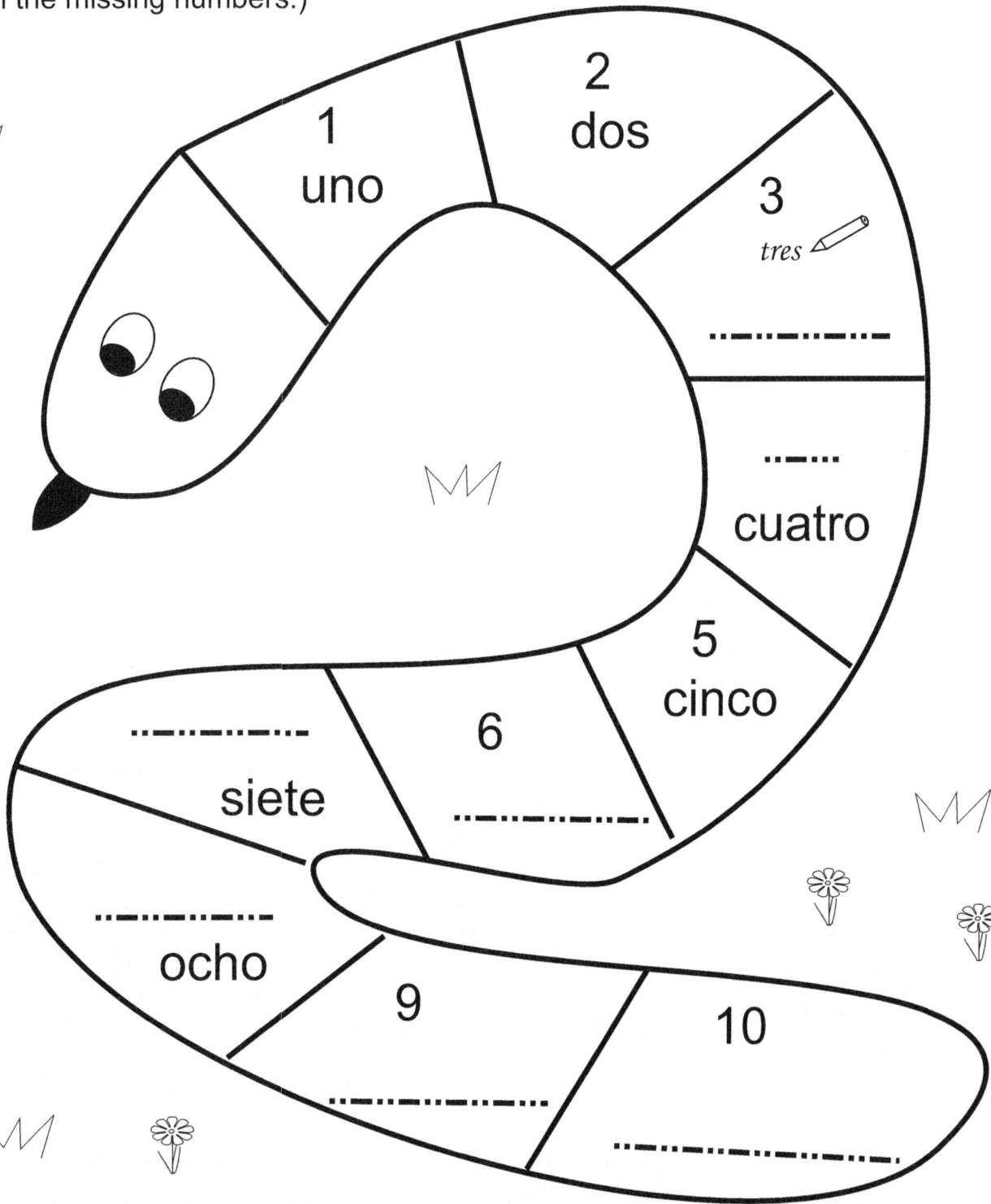

1 uno

2 dos

3 tres

cuatro

5 cinco

6

siete

ocho

9

10

1	2	3	4	5	6	7	8	9	10
uno	dos	tres	cuatro	cinco	seis	siete	ocho	nueve	diez

¿Qué número es? (What number is it?)

Ordena las letras, y escribe la palabra:
(Rearrange the letters, and write the word:)

a)

tres ✏

b)

c)

d)

e)

f)

g)

h)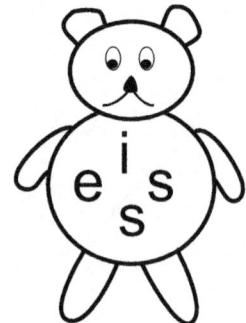

1	2	3	4	5	6	7	8	9	10
uno	dos	tres	cuatro	cinco	seis	siete	ocho	nueve	diez

¿Qué quiere? (What do you want?)

Siete por favor. (seven please.)

Pregunta por la cantidad correcta y di por favor.

(Ask for the quantity shown for each of the following, and then say **por favor.**)
(**Por favor** means please.)

a) *Dos por favor.* ✏️

_____ _____ _____ .

b) _____ _____ _____ .

c) _____ _____ _____ .

d) _____ _____ _____ .

e) _____ _____ _____ .

1	2	3	4	5	6	7	8	9	10
uno	dos	tres	cuatro	cinco	seis	siete	ocho	nueve	diez

¡Sumamos! (Let's add up!)

5 cinco			6 seis
4 cuatro			7 siete
3 tres			8 ocho
2 dos			9 nueve
1 uno			10 diez

a) tres + dos = *cinco*

b) siete - cinco =

c) nueve - uno =

d) seis + cuatro =

e) cinco + tres =

f) diez - seis =

g) ocho + uno =

h) cinco - dos =

i) tres + cuatro =

¿Cuántos años tienes? (How old are you?)

Tengo ___ años. - I am ___ years old.

a) 5

b) 10

c) 8

d) 7

e) 6

f) 9

Tengo cinco años.

a) _____ .

b) _____ .

c) _____ .

d) _____ .

e) _____ .

f) _____ .

5 - cinco
6 - seis
7 - siete
8 - ocho
9 - nueve
10 - diez

Sopa de letras (wordsearch)

Busca los números. (Look for numbers.)

```
U  N  O  B  T  R  D  N  U  E  V  E
R  B  S  S  D  E  O  R  M  G  U  P
N  R  O  G  M  U  H  S  E  I  S  K
E  D  K  N  G  S  T  P  E  L  I  O
O  S  E  R  M  B  D  K  W  E  Z  T
U  D  G  C  U  A  T  R  O  U  E  R
O  C  R  U  E  G  M  L  H  Y  R  E
U  I  O  P  S  M  E  I  T  O  Z  S
G  N  E  R  I  K  L  Z  H  N  I  B
P  C  G  M  E  S  K  C  E  I  W  Z
L  O  E  K  T  M  O  Z  Y  S  T  S
Z  W  G  I  E  T  K  M  D  I  E  Z
```

1	**2**	**3**	**4**	**5**
UNO	DOS	TRES	CUATRO	CINCO

6	**7**	**8**	**9**	**10**
SEIS	SIETE	OCHO	NUEVE	DIEZ

12

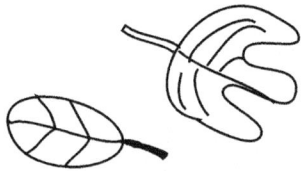

verde

amarillo

rojo

lila

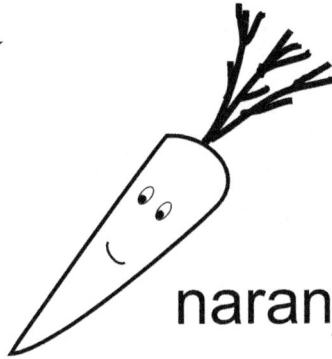

naranja

azul

Los colores

blanco

rosa

marrón

gris

negro

¿De qué color son? (What colour are they?)

verde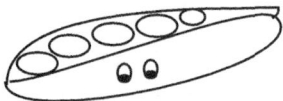

a)

b)

_____

c)

_____

d)

_____

e)

_____

f)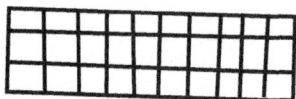

_____

g)

_____

rojo - red   verde - green   amarillo - yellow   gris - grey

naranja - orange   marrón - brown   negro y blanco - black and white

14

Los colores (colours)

Colorea los números usando estos colores:
(Colour the numbers using these colours:)

1 = rojo   2 = azul   3 = verde   4 = amarillo   5 = rosa

6 = lila   7 = blanco   8 = gris   9 = marrón   10 = negro

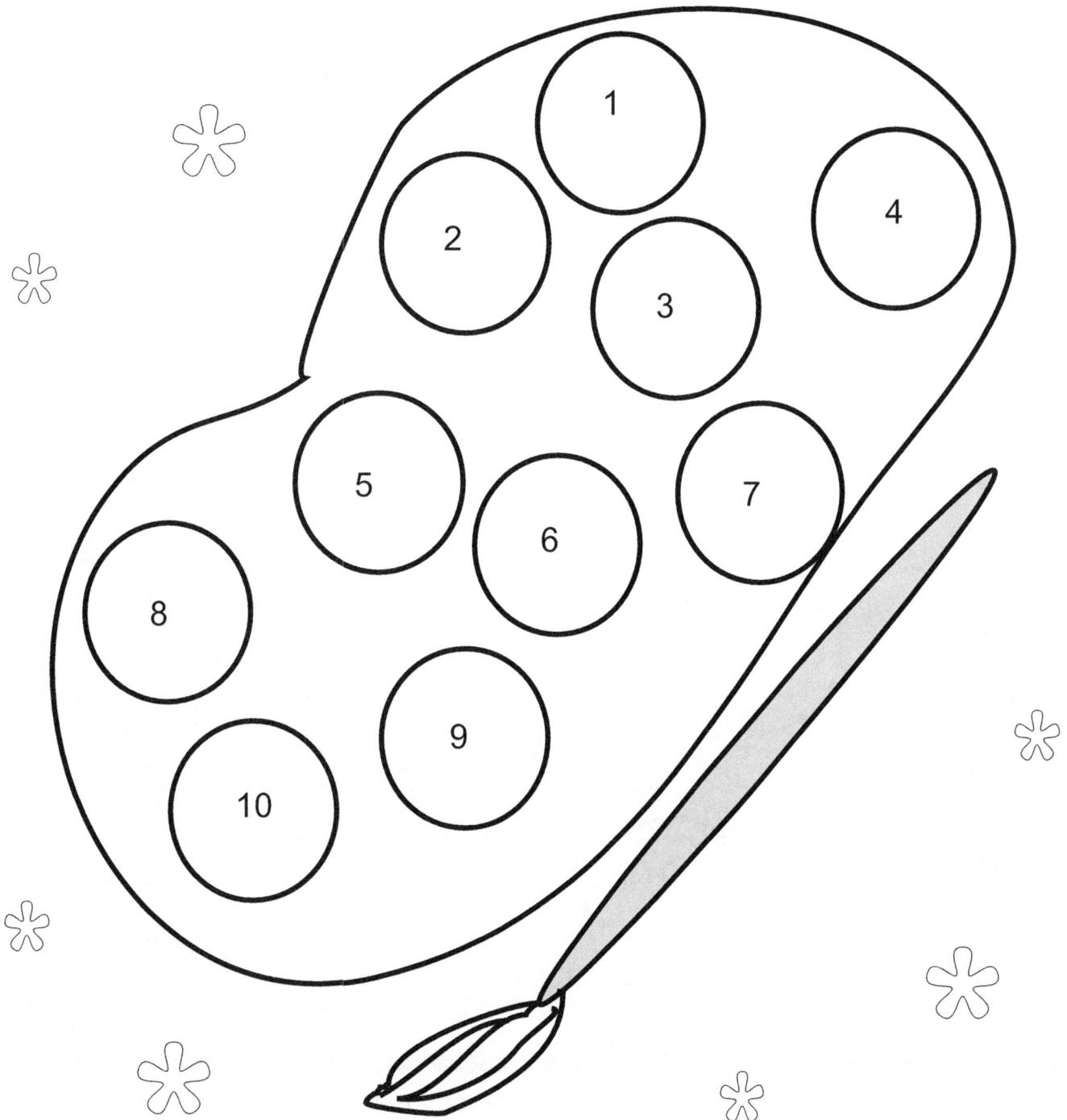

Colorea los balones (Colour the balls)

tres en azul
(3 in blue)

cuatro en verde
(4 in green)

cuatro en rojo

dos en lila

dos en amarillo

tres en rosa

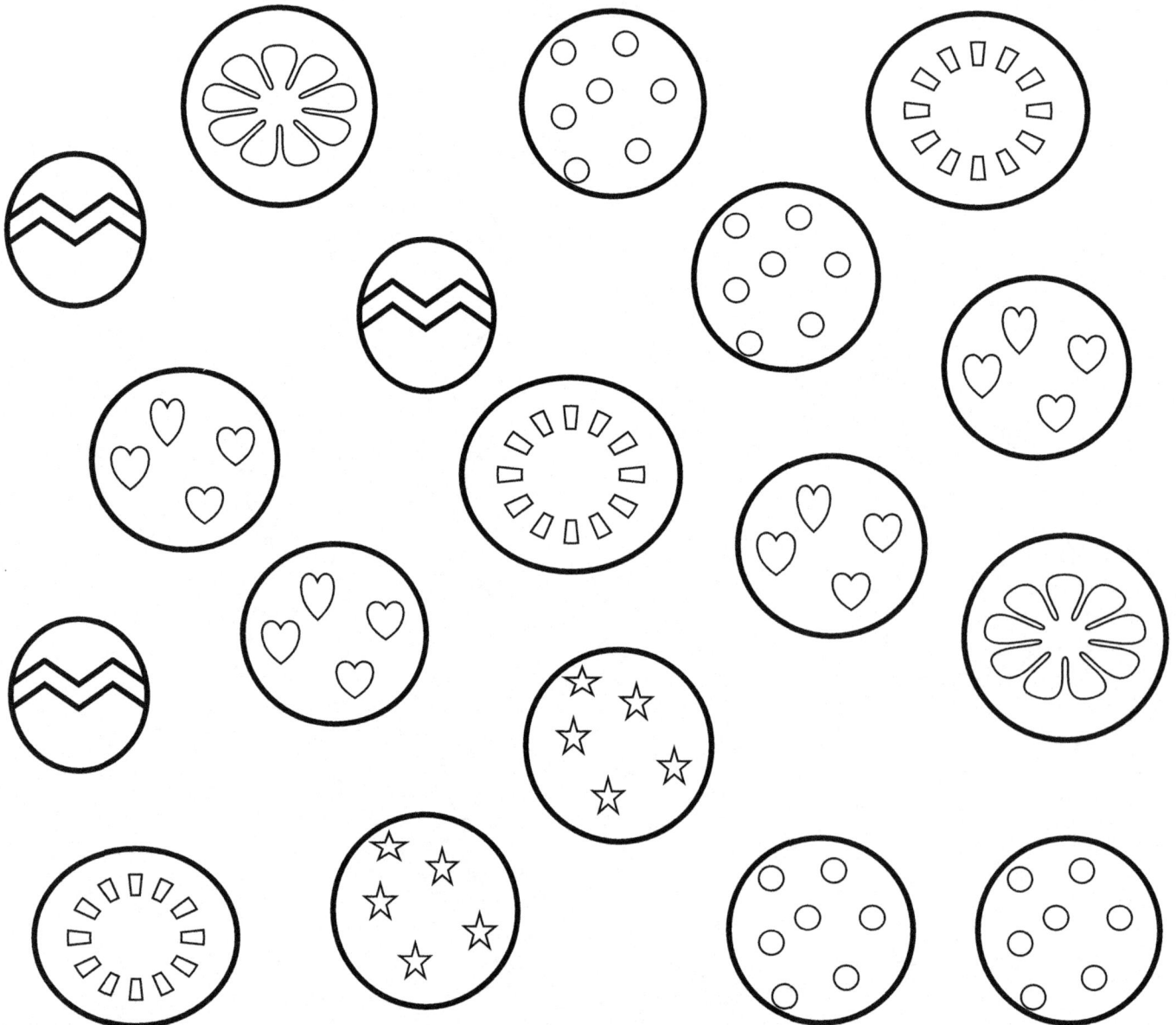

rojo - red   azul - blue   verde - green   amarillo - yellow   lila - lilac   rosa - pink

¿Qué colores te gustan?

(Which colours do you like?)

Me gusta
(I like)

No me gusta
(I don't ike)

		rojo
	el	azul
		verde
		gris
		marrón
		negro

Me gusta el rojo. = I like red.
No me gusta el rojo. = I don't like red.

a) 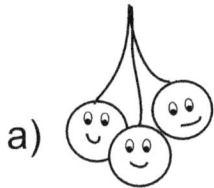 _____ .

b)  _____ .

c)  _____ .

d)  _____ .

e)  _____ .

f)  _____ .

rojo - red   azul - blue   verde - green   gris - grey   marrón - brown   negro - black

Sopa de letras (wordsearch)

Busca estas palabras: (Look for these words:)

VERDE   AMARILLO   ROJO   NEGRO   LILA   ROSA

   NARANJA    BLANCO   MARRÓN   AZUL

GRIS

R	O	J	O	U	E	B	T	A	R	U	D
S	U	T	B	D	R	A	N	Z	E	S	R
T	B	S	R	B	S	K	E	U	D	I	O
R	U	E	S	O	T	D	B	L	O	R	S
N	V	S	R	L	E	R	D	G	R	G	M
M	O	N	D	B	L	A	N	C	O	U	S
A	D	E	S	B	N	M	R	S	U	M	U
R	B	G	U	A	M	A	R	I	L	L	O
R	O	R	U	S	D	B	R	S	N	H	K
Ó	B	O	R	K	Z	W	B	A	L	I	L
N	O	H	N	P	S	Y	L	W	B	Z	Y
D	N	A	R	A	N	J	A	E	B	S	W

una camiseta

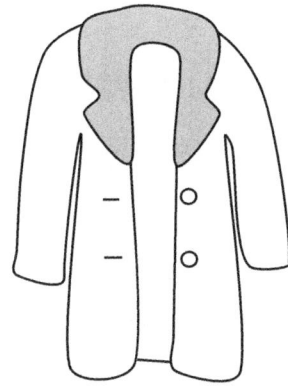

un abrigo

una falda

un jersey

LA ROPA

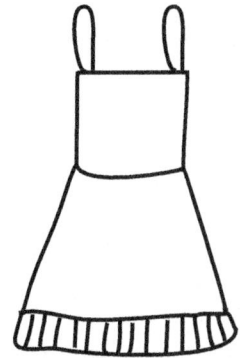

un vestido

unos pantalones cortos

unos vaqueros

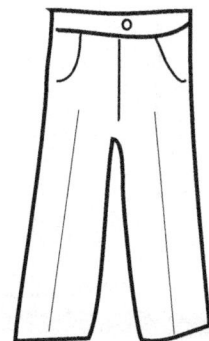

unos pantalones

La moda (fashion)

Imagina que eres modista. Dibuja:
(Imagine you are a fashion designer. Draw:)

una camiseta

unos pantalones

una falda

un jersey

un abrigo

un vestido

unos vaqueros

unos pantalones cortos

un vestido   un jersey   un abrigo   una camiseta   una falda   unos vaqueros   unos pantalones cortos

¿Cuánto cuesta?

(How much does it cost?)

€ 10

€ 6

€ 7

€ 9

€ 8

¿Cuánto cuesta?   (How much does it cost?)

siete

Una falda cuesta _____ euros.

Una camiseta cuesta _____ euros.

Un jersey cuesta _____ euros.

Un abrigo cuesta _____ euros.

Un vestido cuesta _____ euros.

6 - seis   7 - siete   8 - ocho   9 - nueve   10 - diez

¿Cuántos hay? (How many are there?)

a)

cuatro 🖊 _____ camiseta**s**

b)

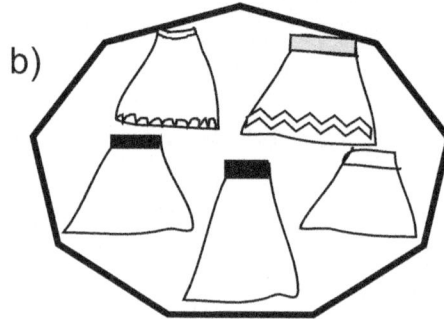

_____ falda**s**

c)

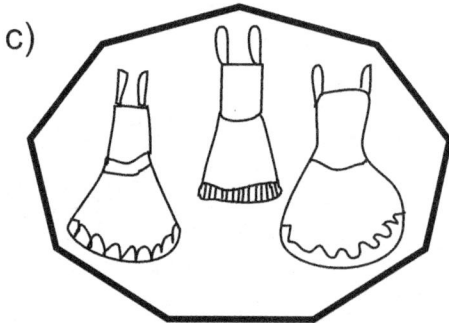

_____ vestido**s**

d)

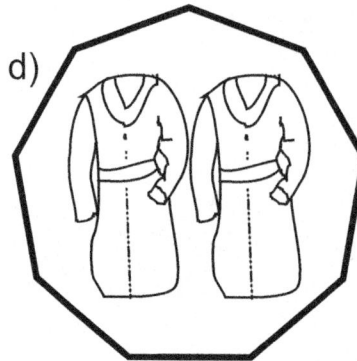

_____ abrigo**s**

f)

_____ camiseta**s**

g)

_____ abrigo**s**

h)

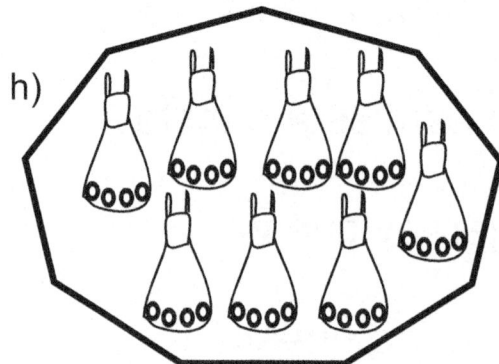

_____ vestido**s**

1	2	3	4	5	6	7	8	9	10
uno	dos	tres	cuatro	cinco	seis	siete	ocho	nueve	diez

¿Qué quiere? (What do you want?)

Pregunta por estas cosas. (Ask for these things.)
Start with **Me gustaría** (I would like) and end with **por favor** (please).

a)  *Me gustaría un jersey por favor.*

_____ .

b)

_____ .

c)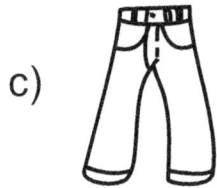

_____ .

d)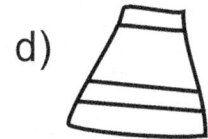

_____ .

e)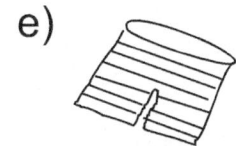

_____ .

f)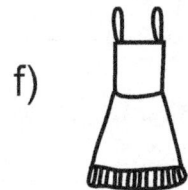

_____ .

g)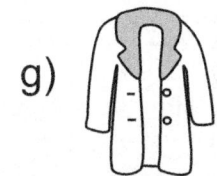

_____ .

un vestido   un jersey   un abrigo   una camiseta   una falda   unos vaqueros   unos pantalones cortos

23

¿De qué color es? (What colour is it?)

Colorea las camisetas con el color adecuado
Colour the t-shirts in the correct colour

una camiseta azul

una camiseta gris

una camiseta lila

una camiseta naranja

una camiseta rosa

una camiseta verde

una camiseta marrón

una camiseta azul y gris

In Spanish notice that the colours go after the noun
e.g una camiseta azul = a blue T-shirt.

And in Spanish is "y"

azul........ blue

verde ..... green

gris........ grey

lila......... lilac

rosa....... pink

naranja... orange

marrón... brown

¿Qué llevas? (What are you wearing?)

Lee las frases y dibuja la ropa que llevan:
(Read the phrases and draw the clothes they are wearing:)

Llevo - I am wearing   y - and

Llevo unos vaqueros y un jersey.

Llevo unos pantalones cortos y una camiseta.

Llevo un vestido.

Llevo una falda y una camiseta.

un vestido   un jersey   una camiseta   una falda   unos vaqueros   unos pantalones cortos

Sopa de letras (wordsearch)

Busca estas palabras. (Look for these words.)

el ABRIGO   el JERSEY   la FALDA   la CAMISETA

los PANTALONES

los PANTALONES CORTOS

los VAQUEROS

el VESTIDO

la ROPA

```
P A N T A L O N E S
W L A T E S I M A C
A Y L W Z L Y E L Z
B V A Q U E R O S O
R E Z E H Y W K Y D
I L Y K A L P E M I
G E W D P N S Y R T
O Z L H U R H K B S
E A K P E S U T S E
F Z E J L R O P A V
```

In Spanish there are four different ways of saying our word "the" : el, la, los, las.
These words do not appear in the word searches.

un pájaro

un gato

un conejo

una serpiente

un caballo

Los animales

un perro

una tortuga

un ratón

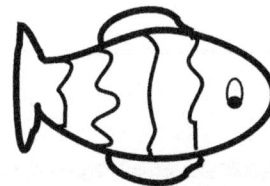

un pez

Los animales

Escribe en español los nombres de los animales.
(Write in Spanish the names of the animals.)

a) *un pez*

b)

_____

_____

c)

d)

_____

_____

e)

f)

_____

g)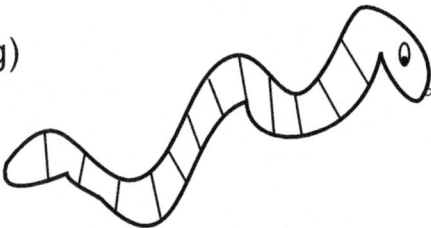

h)

_____

_____

un gato   un perro   un conejo   un pez   un caballo   una serpiente   una tortuga   un pájaro

28

¿Qué animal tienen? (What pet do they have?)

Tengo = I have	Tengo un pez . = I have a fish.

a)

b)

c)

d)

e)

Tengo un pájaro.

a) _____ .

b) _____ .

c) _____ .

d) _____ .

e) _____ .

un gato   un perro   un pez   una tortuga   un pájaro

¿De qué color es? (What colour is it?)

Colorea los animales, usando el color adecuado
(Colour the animals using the correct colour)

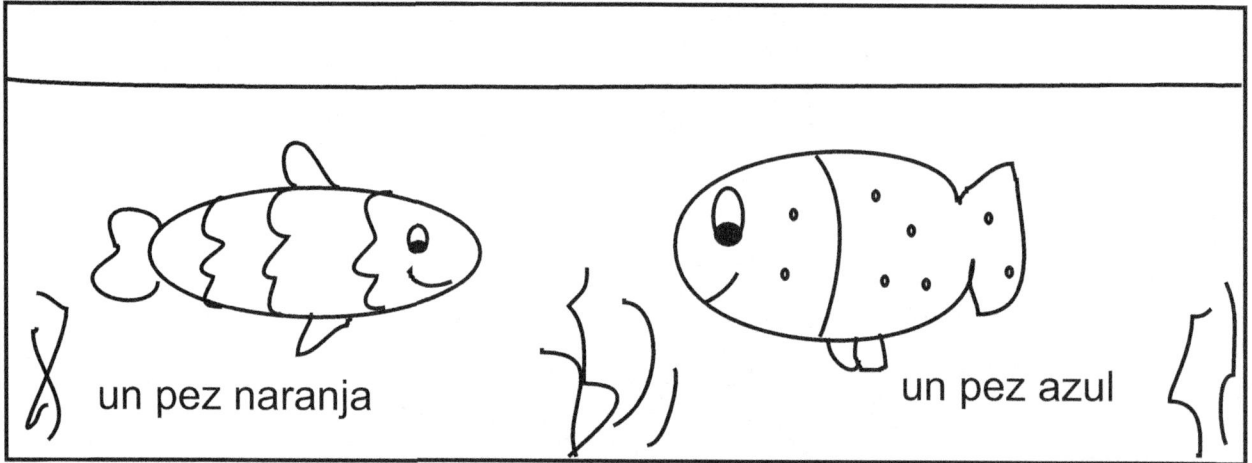

un pez naranja

un pez azul

un pájaro rojo

un perro marrón

un caballo marrón

una serpiente verde

un gato negro

In Spanish notice that the colours go after
the noun e.g un pez naranja = an orange fish.

¿Cómo se llaman? (What are they called?)

1) Elige un nombre para los animales.

(Choose any name for the animals.)

Se llama = It's called

a) Tengo un gato marrón.

Tigger ✏

Se llama _____.

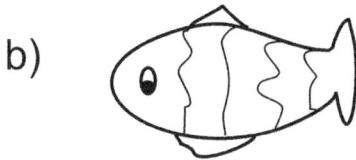

b) Tengo un pez naranja.

Se llama _____.

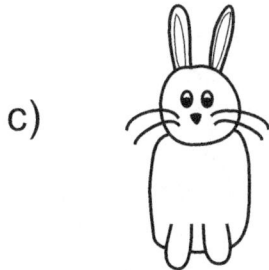

c) Tengo un conejo gris.

Se llama _____.

d) Tengo un perro blanco y negro.

Se llama _____.

e) Tengo un caballo marrón.

Se llama _____.

2) Colorea los animales, usando el color adecuado.

(Colour the animals using the correct colour.)

marrón - brown   naranja - orange   gris - grey   blanco y negro - black and white

¿Es grande o es pequeño? (Is it big or small?)

Es grande
= It's big

Es pequeño
= It's small

a)

Es pequeño. _____.

b)

_____.

c)

_____.

d)

_____.

e)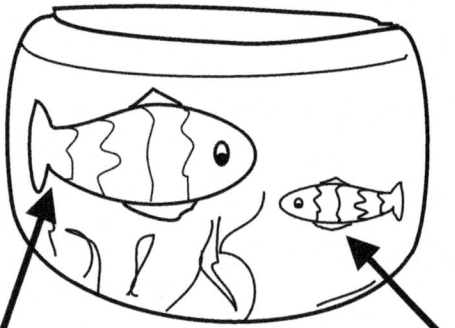

f) _____.

_____.

g)

_____.

h)

_____.

¿Cuántos animales hay?

(How many animals are there?)

cinco ✏️

_____ gato**s**   _____ pájaro**s**

_____ caballo**s**   _____ conejo**s**

_____ tortuga**s**   _____ serpiente**s**

_____ perro**s**

Look at the words for the animals. The words end in **s** because there is more than one of each animal.

1	2	3	4	5	6	7	8
uno	dos	tres	cuatro	cinco	seis	siete	ocho

33

¿Tienes una mascota?

(Do you have a pet?)

¡Hola!

¿Tienes una mascota?

Tengo un gato. Es blanco y es pequeño.

Rosa tiene un conejo. Es gris y es grande.

Antonio tiene un pez. Es naranja y es pequeño.

Ana tiene un caballo. Es marrón y es grande.

Carlos tiene un perro. Es negro y es pequeño.

¡Hasta luego!

María

¿Quién tiene? (Who has ....?)

a) A dog _____

b) A pet which is orange and small _____

c) A rabbit _____

d) A pet which is brown and big _____

e) A fish _____

f) A pet which is black and small _____

Sopa de letras (wordsearch)

Busca estas palabras. (Look for these words.)

el PERRO

el CABALLO

el PEZ

el CONEJO

el PÁJARO

el GATO

la SERPIENTE

la TORTUGA

el HÁMSTER

el RATÓN

```
S E R P I E N T E C
B T R O N G M U P O
O E T D O P R S G N
R A B R M U S R E E
G S R B R A T Ó N J
M E B P Á J A R O O
P M O L L A B A C R
R S R B D G U R G P
S T O R T U G A O E
H Á M S T E R B G Z
```

In Spanish there are four
different ways of saying
our word "the" : el, la, los, las.
These words do not appear in the word search.

Llueve

Hace sol

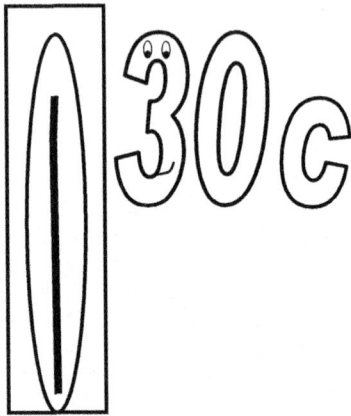

Hace calor

Hace frío

Nieva

El tiempo

Hace buen tiempo

Hace mal tiempo

El tiempo (weather)

Copia las palabras y haz un dibujo.
(Copy the words and draw a picture.)

 Llueve

Llueve ✏

_____

 Hace sol

_____

 Hace frío

_____

 Hace calor

_____

 Hace buen tiempo

_____

 Hace mal tiempo

_____

¿Qué tiempo hace? (What's the weather like?)

Lee las frases y haz los dibujos.
(Read the phrases and draw the pictures.)

Hace frío

Llueve

Hace mal tiempo

Nieva

Hace buen tiempo

Hace calor

Hace sol

¿Qué tiempo hace? (What's the weather like?)

Lee las frases y haz los dibujos.
(Read the phrases and draw the pictures.)

Lunes (Monday)	hace calor
Martes (Tuesday)	hace sol
Miércoles (Wednesday)	llueve
Jueves (Thursday)	hace frío
Viernes (Friday)	hace mal tiempo
Sábado (Saturday)	nieva
Domingo (Sunday)	hace buen tiempo

lunes

martes

miércoles

jueves

viernes

sábado

domingo

In Spanish the days of the week only have a capital letter at the start of a sentence or when they are in a list.

Sopa de letras (word search)

Busca estas palabras. (Look for these words.)

SOL

LLUEVE

MAL TIEMPO

BUEN TIEMPO

0 c
FRÍO

30 c
CALOR

VIERNES

SÁBADO

DOMINGO

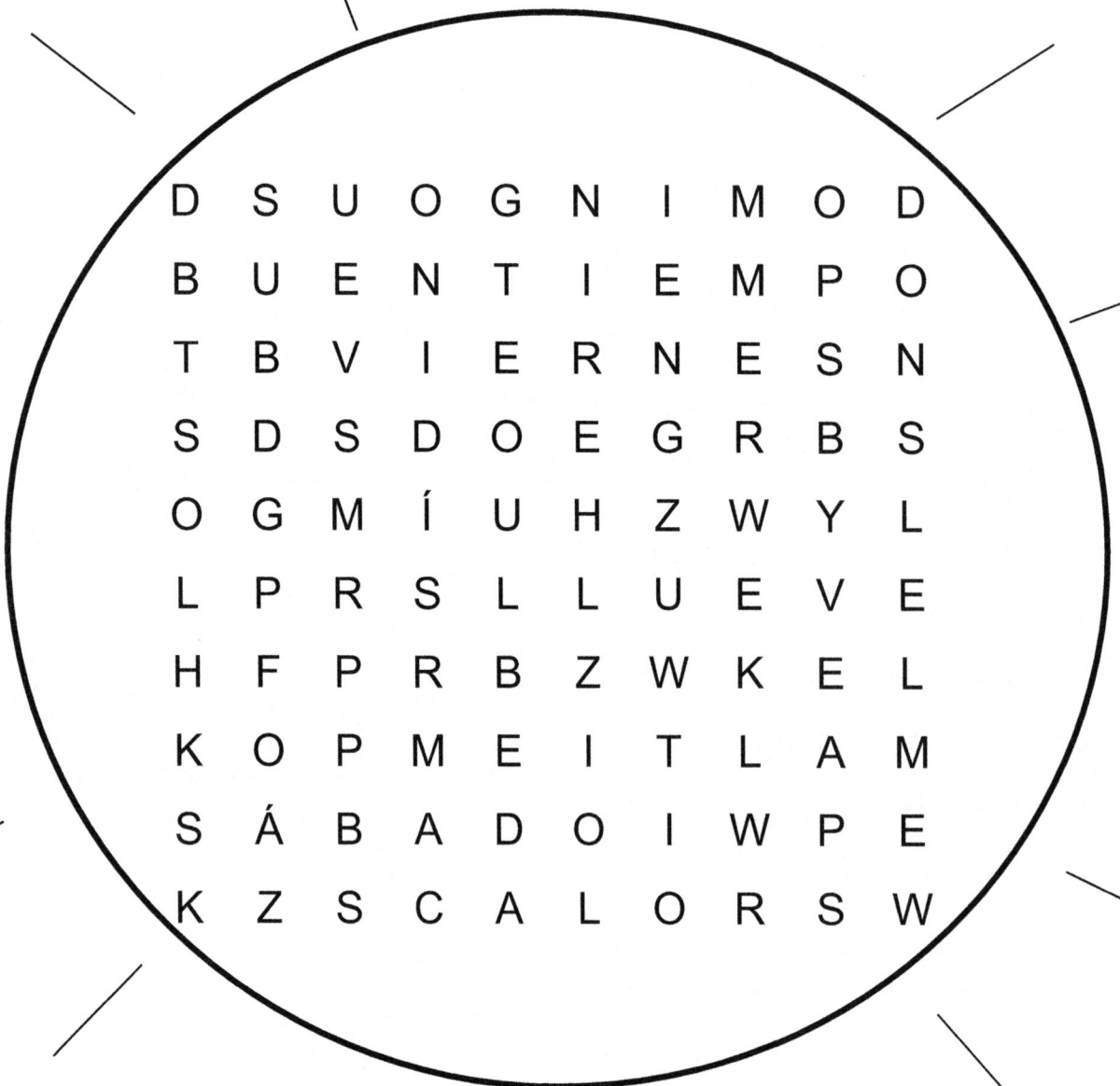

```
D  S  U  O  G  N  I  M  O  D
B  U  E  N  T  I  E  M  P  O
T  B  V  I  E  R  N  E  S  N
S  D  S  D  O  E  G  R  B  S
O  G  M  Í  U  H  Z  W  Y  L
L  P  R  S  L  L  U  E  V  E
H  F  P  R  B  Z  W  K  E  L
K  O  P  M  E  I  T  L  A  M
S  Á  B  A  D  O  I  W  P  E
K  Z  S  C  A  L  O  R  S  W
```

Spanish word		English word	
un	abrigo	a	coat
	adiós		goodbye
	amarillo		yellow
los	animales		animals
	años		years
	azul		blue
los	balones	the	balls
	blanco		white
	Buenas noches		Good night
	Buenas tardes		Good afternoon
	Buenos días		Good morning
un	caballo	a	horse
	caballos		horses
una	camiseta	a	T-shirt
	camisetas		T-shirts
la	cantidad		quantity
	cinco		five
los	colores	the	colours
	¿Cómo estás?		How are you?
	¿Cómo te llamas?		What is your name?
un	conejo	a	rabbit
	¿Cuánto cuesta?		How much is it?
	¿Cuántos?		How many?
	cuatro		four
	cuesta		it costs
	dibuja		draw
un	dibujo	a	picture
los	dibujos	the	pictures
	diez		ten
	dos		two
	en		in
	en español		in Spanish
	es		is
	español		Spanish
una	falda	a	skirt
	faldas		skirts
las	frases	the	phrases
un	gato	a	cats
	gracias		thank you
	grande		big
	gris		grey
	hace buen tiempo		it's good weather
	hace calor		it's hot
	hace frío		it's cold
	hace mal tiempo		it's bad weather
	hace sol		it's sunny
	hasta luego		see you

Spanish word		English word	
	mal		bad
	marrón		brown
	me gusta		I Like
	me gustaría		I would like
	me llamo		My name is
la	moda	the	fashion
	modista		fashion designer
	muy bien		very good
	naranja		orange
	negro		black
	nieva		it's snowing
los	niños		the children
	no		no
	no me gusta		I don't like
	no tengo		I don't have
los	nombres	the	names
	nueve		nine
el	número		number
los	números		numbers
	ocho		eight
un	pájaro	a	bird
la	palabra	the	word
unos	pantalones	some	trousers
unos	pantalones cortos	some	shorts
	peces		fishes
	pequeño		small
un	perro	a	dog
	perros		dogs
las	personas		the people
un	pez	a	fish
	por favor		please
	¿Qué llevas?		What are you wearing?
	¿Qué quiere?		What do you want?
	¿Qué...?		What …?
	regular		so so
	rojo		red
la	ropa		clothes
	rosa		pink
	se llama		he / she is called
	seis		six
una	serpiente	a	snake
	sí		yes
	siete		seven
	sopa de letras		word search
	tengo		I have
el	tiempo		the weather
	¿Tienes....?		Do you have....?

Llegada

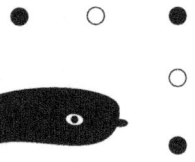

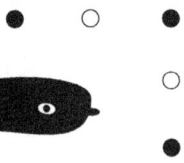

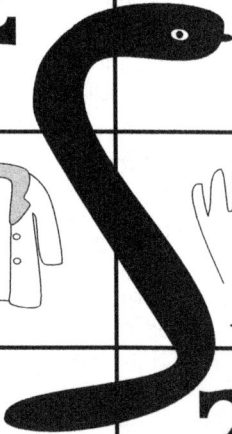

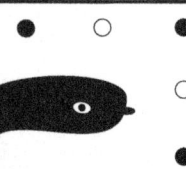

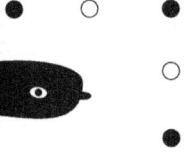

Salida

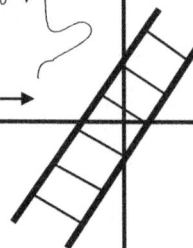

Snakes & ladders game

How to play

Start at **Salida**, roll the dice and count that number of squares.

If the final square has the bottom of the ladder in it go up it, or if it has the head of a snake go down it.

Say the Spanish word for the picture you land on.

To win, arrive first at **Llegada**.

Useful Spanish words

Hola
(Hello)

Adiós
(Goodbye)

1

uno
(one)

2

dos
(two)

un gato
(a cat)

un perro
(a dog)

una camiseta
(a t-shirt)

un abrigo
(a coat)

Games are a fun way to learn a foreign language! If you like games you could try the book: Spanish Word Games - Cool Kids Speak Spanish

Answers

Page 2

2a) Me llamo Carlos   b) Me llamo Rosa   c) Me llamo Juan
d) Me llamo Carmen   e) Me llamo Antonio

Page 3

a) regular   b) my bien   c) mal   d) muy bien   e) mal
f) regular   g) regular   h) mal

Page 4

a) adiós = goodbye   b) Buenas tardes = Good afternoon
c) por favor = please   d) gracias = thank you

Page 5

B	U	E	N	O	S	D	Í	A	S		B
	Í										U
S		M	E	L	L	A	M	O			E
			M	U	Y	B	I	E	N		N
											A
B	U	E	N	A	S	N	O	C	H	E	S
								A	T
	R	E	G	U	L	A	R		L		A
M			O					O			R
A		N				H					D
L	H	A	S	T	A	L	U	E	G	O	E
		A	D	I	Ó	S					S

Page 7

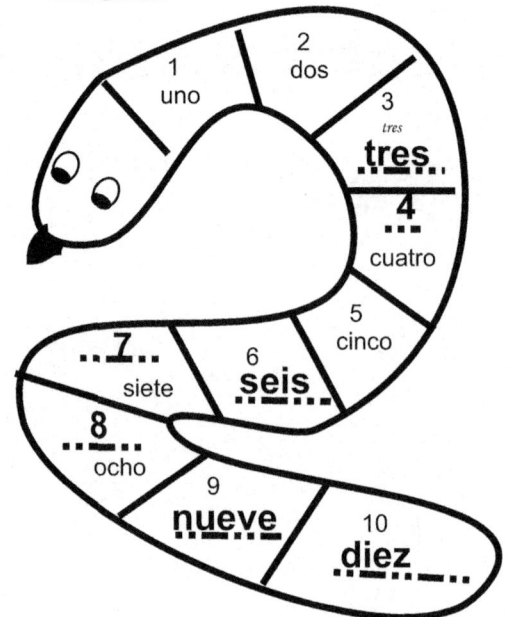

1 uno
2 dos
3 tres
4 cuatro
5 cinco
6 seis
7 siete
8 ocho
9 nueve
10 diez

Page 8

a) tres   b) dos   c) diez   d) uno
e) cinco   f) cuatro   g) nueve   h) seis

Page 9

a) dos por favor   b) cuatro por favor   c) seis por favor
d) cinco por favor   e) tres por favor

Page 10

a) cinco   b) dos   c) ocho   d) diez   e) ocho   f) cuatro
g) nueve   h) tres   i) siete

Page 11

a) Tengo cinco años   b) Tengo diez años   c) Tengo ocho años
d) Tengo siete años   e) Tengo seis años   f) Tengo nueve años

Page 12

U	N	O					N	U	E	V	E
		S									
		O					S	E	I	S	
D											
											T
		C	U	A	T	R	O				R
C											E
I		S					O		S		
N		I			H						
C		E		C							
O		T		O							
		E			D	I	E	Z			

Page 14
a) verde   b) rojo   c) naranja   d) amarillo
e) gris   f) marrón   g) negro y blanco

Page 15
1 = red   2 = blue   3 = green   4 = yellow   5 = pink
6 = lilac   7 = white   8 = grey   9 = brown   10 = black

Page 16

3 in blue   4 in red   two in yellow
4 in green   two in lilac   three in pink

Page 17

If you like the colours:
a) Me gusta el rojo
b) Me gusta el verde
c) Me gusta el gris
d) Me gusta el negro
e) Me gusta el marrón
f) Me gusta el azul

If you don't like the colours:
No me gusta el rojo
No me gusta el verde
No me gusta el gris
No me gusta el negro
No me gusta el marrón
No me gusta el azul

R	O	J	O		E			A			
				D		A		Z		S	
			R		S			U		I	
		E		O				L		R	
	V		R							G	
M		N		B	L	A	N	C	O		
A		E									
R		G		A	M	A	R	I	L	L	O
R		R									
Ó		O					A	L	I	L	
N											
	N	A	R	A	N	J	A				

Page 20

una camiseta = a T-shirt   unos pantalones = trousers   una falda = a skirt
un jersey = a jumper   unos pantalones cortos = shorts
unos vaqueros = jeans   un abrigo = a coat   un vestido = a dress

Page 21

a) siete   b) seis   c) ocho   d) diez   e) nueve

Page 22

a) cuatro   b) cinco   c) tres   d) dos   e) siete   f) cinco   g) ocho

Page 23

a) Me gustaría un jersey por favor.
b) Me gustaría una camiseta por favor.
c) Me gustaría unos vaqueros por favor.
d) Me gustaría una falda por favor.
e) Me gustaría unos pantalones cortos por favor.
f) Me gustaría un vestido por favor.
g) Me gustaría un abrigo por favor.

Page 24

una camiseta azul = a blue T-shirt   una camiseta gris = a grey T-shirt
una camiseta lila = a lilac T-shirt   una camiset naranja = an orange T-shirt
una camiseta rosa = a pink T-shirt   una camiseta verde = a green T-shirt
una camiseta marrón = a brown T-shirt
una camiseta azul y gris = a blue and grey T-shirt

Page 25

Llevo un vestido = I am wearing a dress
Llevo unos vaqueros y un jersey = I am wearing some jeans and a jumper
Llevo una falda y una camiseta = I am wearing a skirt and a T-shirt
Llevo unos pantalones cortos y una camiseta = I am wearing shorts and a T-shirt

Page 26

P	A	N	T	A	L	O	N	E	S
	A	T	E	S	I	M	A	C	
A									
B	V	A	Q	U	E	R	O	S	O
R								Y	D
I			A			E			I
G		D			S				T
O		L		R					S
	A		E						E
F			J		R	O	P	A	V

Page 28

a) un pez   b) un caballo   c) un conejo
d) un perro   e) un gato   f) un pájaro
g) una serpiente   h) una tortuga

Page 29

a) Tengo un pájaro   b) Tengo un gato
c) Tengo un pez   d) Tengo un perro
e) Tengo una tortuga

Page 30

The animals should be coloured as follows:

un pez naranja = an orange fish   un pez azul = a blue fish
un pájaro rojo = a red bird   un perro marrón = a brown dog
un caballo marrón = a brown horse   una serpiente verde = a green snake
un gato negro = a black cat

Page 31

After se llama you can have written any name you chose for the pet
The animals should be coloured as follows:

un gato marrón = a brown cat   un pez naranja = an oragne fish
un conejo gris = a grey rabbit   un perro blanco y negro = a black & white dog
un caballo marrón = a brown horse

Page 32

a) Es pequeño   b) Es grande   c) Es pequeño   d) Es grande
e) Es grande   f) Es pequeño   g) Es pequeño   h) Es grande

Page 33

cinco gatos   seis pájaros
tres caballos   siete conejos
cuatro tortugas   tres serpientes
dos perros

Page 34

a) Carlos   d) Ana
b) Antonio   e) Antonio
c) Rosa   d) Carlos

Page 35

S	E	R	P	I	E	N	T	E	C
	O								O
	T		O						N
	A		R						E
G	R		R	A	T	Ó	N		J
	E		P	Á	J	A	R	O	O
P	O		L	L	A	B	A	C	
									P
	T		O	R	T	U	G	A	E
H	Á		M	S	T	E	R		Z

Page 39

Pictures for the weather should be as follows:

Lunes   - It's hot
Martes   - It's sunny
Miércoles - It's raining
Jueves - It's cold
Viernes - It's bad weather
Sábado - It's snowing
Domingo - It's good weather

Page 38

Hace frío = It's cold
Hace mal tiempo = It's bad weather
Hace buen tiempo = It's good weather
Llueve = It's raining
Nieva = It's snowing
Hace calor = It's hot
Hace sol = It's sunny

Page 40

				O	G	N	I	M	O	D
B	U	E	N	T	I	E	M	P	O	
		V	I	E	R	N	E	S		
S				O						
O			Í							
L		R		L	L	U	E	V	E	
	F									
		O	P	M	E	I	T	L	A	M
S	Á	B	A	D	O					
		C	A	L	O	R				

I hope you have enjoyed the fun activities in this book! Try to look back at the Spanish words from time to time to help you remember them.

Reviews help other readers discover my books so please consider leaving a short review on the site where the book was purchased. Your feedback is important to me.

Thank you! And have fun learning Spanish! It's a lovely language to learn!

Joanne Leyland

For more information about learning Spanish and the great books by Joanne Leyland go to **https://funspanishforkids.com**

For information about learning French, Spanish, German, Italian or English as a foreign language go to **https://learnforeignwords.com**

For children aged 7-11 there are also the following books by Joanne Leyland:

Cool Kids Speak Spanish - Books 1, 2 and 3

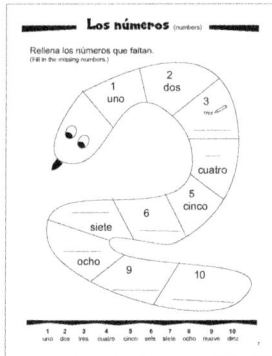

With 6 interesting topics in every book. Each topic starts with an introductory picture page showing all the words for that topic. These words are then practised, and sentences are built using the words. The topics end with a fun word search.

On Holiday In Spain
Cool Kids Speak Spanish

Ideal for holidays and to challenge children to speak Spanish whilst away. Topics include greetings, numbers, drinks, food, souvenirs, town, hotels & campsites.

Photocopiable Games For Teaching Spanish

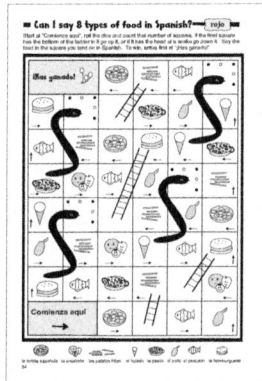

Differentiated activities for children of various abilities. The games are colour coded according to the amount of Spanish words in each game.

40 Spanish Word Searches
Cool Kids Speak Spanish

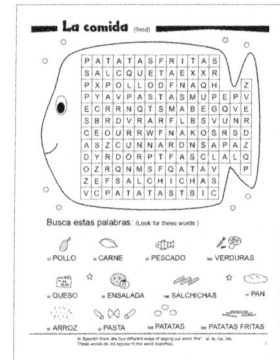

The word searches appear in fun shapes and pictures accompany the Spanish words so that each word search can be a meaningful learning activity. 40 Topics.

First 100 Words In Spanish Coloring Book - Cool Kids Speak Spanish

The 100 Spanish words in this brilliant book include a marvellous mix of favourite children's characters (for example a fairy, a dragon, a mermaid, a dinosaur or a unicorn) and useful Spanish words like some food, types of transport, animals, toys and clothes. The 30 delightful pages all have borders and are single sided.

For more information about learning Spanish and the great books by Joanne Leyland go to **https://funspanishforkids.com**

French
Also available by Joanne Leyland

Young Cool Kids Learn French
French Colouring Book For Kids Ages 5 - 7
First Words In French Teacher's Resource Book
Stories for 3-7 year olds: Jack And The French Languasaurus - Books 1, 2 & 3,
Daniel And The French Robot - Books 1, 2 & 3, Sophie And The French Magician
Cool Kids Speak French - Books 1, 2 & 3 *(for kids ages 7 - 11)*
French Word Games - Cool Kids Speak French
Photocopiable Games For Teaching French
40 French Word Searches Cool Kids Speak French
First 100 Words In French Coloring Book Cool Kids Speak French
French at Christmas time
On Holiday In France Cool Kids Speak French
Cool Kids Do Maths In French
Stories in French: Un Alien Sur La Terre, Le Singe Qui Change De Couleur, Tu As Un Animal?

Italian

Young Cool Kids Learn Italian
Italian Colouring Book For Kids Ages 5 - 7
Cool Kids Speak Italian - Books 1, 2 & 3 *(for kids ages 7 - 11)*
Italian Word Games - Cool Kids Speak Italian
Photocopiable Games For Teaching Italian
40 Italian Word Searches Cool Kids Speak Italian
First 100 Words In Italian Coloring Book Cool Kids Speak Italian
On Holiday In Italy Cool Kids Speak Italian
Stories in Italian: Un Alieno Sulla Terra, La Scimmia Che Cambia Colore, Hai Un Animale Domestico?

German

Young Cool Kids Learn German
German Colouring Book For Kids Ages 5 - 7
Sophie And The German Magician *(a story for 3-7 year olds)*
Cool Kids Speak German - Books 1, 2 & 3 *(for kids ages 7 - 11)*
German Word Games - Cool Kids Speak German
Photocopiable Games For Teaching German
40 German Word Searches Cool Kids Speak German
First 100 Words In German Coloring Book Cool Kids Speak German

Spanish

Young Cool Kids Learn Spanish
Spanish Colouring Book For Kids Ages 5 - 7
First Words In Spanish Teacher's Resource Book
Stories for 3-7 year olds: Jack And The Spanish Dinosaur, Sophie And The Spanish Magician,
Daniel And The Spanish Robot - Books 1, 2 & 3
Cool Kids Speak Spanish - Books 1, 2 & 3 *(for kids ages 7 - 11)*
Spanish Word Games - Cool Kids Speak Spanish
Photocopiable Games For Teaching Spanish
40 Spanish Word Searches Cool Kids Speak Spanish
First 100 Words In Spanish Coloring Book Cool Kids Speak Spanish
Spanish at Christmas time
On Holiday In Spain Cool Kids Speak Spanish
Cool Kids Do Maths In Spanish
Stories: Un Extraterrestre En La Tierra, El Mono Que Cambia De Color, Seis Mascotas Maravillosas

English as a second language / foreign language

English For Kids Ages 5 - 7
English Colouring Book For Children Ages 3 - 7
Cool Kids Speak English - Books 1, 2 & 3 *(for kids ages 7 - 11)*
First Words In English - 100 Words To Colour & Learn
English Word Games
Fun Word Search Puzzles

Printed in Great Britain
by Amazon